DRY ROT

THE BEAST
IN THE
BASEMENT

DRY ROT

THE BEAST
IN THE
BASEMENT

Peter Barber
M.I.W.Sc.. C.R.D.S.

Lennard Publishing

First published in 1993 by
Lennard Publishing
a division of Lennard Associates Ltd
Mackerye End
Harpenden
Herts AL5 5DR

ISBN 1 85291 118 2

British Library Cataloguing in Publication Data
is available

Cover design by Forest Publication Services
Line drawings by Alexandra Barber
Photographs by Reflections

Printed and bound in Great Britain by
The Ipswich Book Company

CONTENTS

Introduction

7

The History of Dry Rot

11

What is Dry Rot?

19

How to Recognise Dry Rot

33

How to Treat Dry Rot

59

My Professional Opinion

73

INTRODUCTION

Dry rot is a term that will strike fear into the heart of all home owners. This is largely because of a lack of understanding. When confronted by a dry rot problem, most house owners will refer to a DIY manual in a vain attempt to gain some knowledge of the subject. However if they can find any reference to dry rot, it will be a very sketchy few lines which will not educate but merely advise you that "dry rot can only be dealt with by a specialist." Unfortunately, due to the public's ignorance of the subject, a minority of unscrupulous specialist companies are able to charge unreasonably high prices for small amounts of work.

In writing this book, I will lay down in plain and simple terms:

1. How to recognise and cope with a dry rot outbreak.
2. The causes and history of the fungus.

My aim is to provide readers with the knowledge required to save themselves a fortune in remedial treatment costs.

I must, at this stage, make it quite clear that I do not recommend that *all* dry rot treatments be carried out by the home owners themselves. This book will help in the diagnosis of a fungus, but specialist help must be sought for larger outbreaks. All chemicals used for DIY treatment of dry rot are toxic and, in my opinion, should not be used to treat large areas of fungal infestation without proper training. The treatment of small outbreaks of dry rot should be within the average householder's capability, providing the manufacturer's instructions for correct use of the chemical (which will always be found on the side of the bottle) are strictly followed, as well as the warnings about health and safety. This book should provide enough knowledge to realise when specialist help is required.

The most important aspect of dry rot treatment is early detection, as this fungus will usually show small tell-tale symptoms quite early within its development, which if recognised in good time will make the whole procedure considerably less painful. To illustrate this point, here is a true case history.

I was asked to carry out an inspection of a house near my office for a suspected woodworm outbreak. Mrs Evans greeted me and after checking my business card ushered me inside and down a long passage way into the dining room, where her husband was sipping tea. A strong mushroom odour pervaded the air. They pushed a steaming mug of tea across the table.

"Is it woodworm?" Mr Evans asked pointing to a drop in the floor to one side of the room.

At that moment, I wished I had their optimism. Experience however told me something else.

Not wishing to voice my fears until a sub-floor inspection was carried out, I asked that I may be permitted to look, Mr Evans smiled and waved his tea mug in the direction of the collapsing corner and said: "Help yourself, son."

As I rolled back the carpet, the mushroom smell became stronger, the floor boards were distorted and breaking. I removed enough of the rotted wood to allow a torch and mirror to be lowered under the floors, then it was visible. A mass of white mycelium, like cotton wool, filled the cavity. The under sides of the floorboards were covered in one giant sporiphore which extended as far as I could see. This truly was a major dry rot outbreak.

After explaining to the unsuspecting homeowners the seriousness of the problem, and many tears later, I proceeded to determine the full extent of the fungal outbreak and to estimate the costs involved in the treatment and cure.

The survey at that property took over a day and a half, the whole ground floor consisting of four large rooms. The hallway and staircase were ultimately found to be severely affected, together with two bedrooms and the bathroom on the first floor. The scale of the attack was surprising as the fungus was not showing many surface signs characteristic of the dry rot fungus, but all concealed

Sheets of mycelium affecting joists to the ceiling of an unventilated basement.

areas were severely affected, resulting in terrible damage to almost all areas of the property.

The subsequent cost of works carried out within the property totalled over £10,000 and could well have been avoided by the small amount of knowledge needed to recognise the tell-tale signs of the most damaging fungus, dry rot.

THE HISTORY OF DRY ROT

And God said unto Noah: "Make thee an ark of gopher wood; rooms shalt thou make in the ark; and thou shalt pitch within and without with pitch."

From the dawn of history dry rot has been known to be a problem to affect timber subjected to dampness, thus the instructions given to Noah, which required the use of pitch on the inside of the ark as well as outside.

The earliest biblical reference to dry rot can be found in the book of Leviticus, Chapter XIV, verses 33-57.

The following reference seems to confirm the presence of dry rot in the time of Moses.

"And the Lord spake unto Moses and unto Aaron, saying, when ye be come into the land of Canaan, which I give to you for a possession, and I put the plague of leprosy in a house of the land of your possession; And he that owneth the house shall come and tell the priest, saying, It seemeth to me that there is as it were a plague in the house..."

This passage goes on to indicate the treatment required for this infection which will include stripping away the infected material and casting the stones into an unclean place (this will in effect expose the full infestation). The priest will then lock up the house for seven days, after which, if clear, recommend re-plastering, if the 'leprosy' has spread, then the house will be demolished and the stones taken from the city.

Some scholars seem to assume that this infection was due to insects known as stone worms which lived on the stones, eating away the damp parts. This is certainly a possibility, but references further in the passage describe the colours of the 'leprosy' to be greenish or reddish, which could indicate the colour of the fruiting body and the mycelium, making it more likely to be a fungal infestation.

The problem with this theory is that dry rot fungus is not known in that part of the world due to the crucial temperature requirement. However, it is known that dry rot does not exist outside. We can therefore assume that this fungus evolved with the human race and is therefore subject to change as indeed we are, to suit it's environment. This question will probably remain a mystery for all time.

Dry rot has been known by various names throughout history. This can be confusing when researching in old writings. To avoid confusion, I have set out below all of the names which are known.

Prior to the seventeenth century, all writings refer to 'distemper of wood' . This seems to have described all wood-rotting fungi affecting ships. During the eighteenth century, dry rot was known as *Boletus lacrymans*, which today we know of as a glutenous mushroom that grows in forests and is associated with oak and beech. This name was changed to *Merulius lacrymans* and was recognised as such through the war years until the 1960s, when the name was changed again to *Serpula lacrymans*, the name used today.

The following account of dry rot in ships is compiled with the aid of a most interesting book called *Mushrooms and Toadstools* by Dr Ramsbottom. He retired after 40 years service in the department of Botany at the Natural History Museum, and made a particular study of the history of dry rot.

In the days when all war ships were constructed of wood, dry rot threatened the security of this country.

When Queen Elizabeth 1 came to the throne, she found that 10 out of 32 of her royal ships were unserviceable due to rot.

In history, the greatest threat was thought to be from hostile foreign countries. Unbeknown to our navy, however, a greater threat was developing beneath their very feet! A threat that couldn't be seen until it was too late. A threat that was hell bent on destroying our very ability to defend ourselves.

An interesting account comes from the writings of Samuel Pepys who, whilst on a visit to Chatham, wrote:

"The greatest part of these 30 ships (without having to

look out of harbour) were let to sink into such distress through decay contracted... that several of them lie in danger of sinking at their very moorings, the planks were perished to powder, their holds not cleared or aired have suffered to heat and moulder until I have with my own hands gathered toadstools growing in the most considerable of them, as big as my fist."

Lord Sandwich visited ships in reserve in 1771, before which masses of fungus had to be dug out before the timbers could be inspected.

During the American War of Independence, 66 ships of the Royal Navy sunk. This was thought to be due to the ravages of dry rot.

The design of warships was always limited to the size and quality of the timber available. The HMS *Victory* was built using seasoned oak and was 40 years old at the battle of Trafalgar. In those days, the good policy adopted was to build only a few ships each year, thus ensuring the availability of properly seasoned timbers. It was recommended that good oak should be seasoned for one year per inch thickness. During this time good ship-building oak was known to be at a premium. Admiral Collingwood, a great friend of Lord Nelson, and commander of The *Excellent*, recognised this and planted groves of oak on his estate in Northumberland. He remarked:

"If the country gentlemen do not make a point to plant oaks, the time will not be very distant when to keep our navy, we must depend entirely on captures from the enemy... I wish everybody thought on this subject as I do, they would not walk through their farms without a pocket full of acorns to drop them in the hedge sides, and then let them take their chance."

When war ended and peace resumed, the need for trained ship-builders diminished and shipwrights were discharged. Battleships were no longer needed in such great number and were therefore placed in reserve. The ships were left in dock unventilated and fast became completely unserviceable. This became known as 'Rotten Row'

The *Queen Charlotte,* a first rate with 110 guns was launched in 1810 but rotted even before she was commissioned. Repairs up until 1816 had amounted to £94,499, this is in addition to the original building cost of £88,534. By 1859 the total cost of repairs had amounted to £287,837, when her name was ironically changed to *Excellent.* She was finally broken in 1892.

When war broke out again, although on paper our navy was strong with numerous fighting ships, in reality the rot had affected so many that the size of our fighting force was seriously diminished. Hurriedly, war ships were built from unseasoned timber and put to sea, and promptly rotted. The life expectancy of these new ships was found to be less than 3 years.

The main reason why dry rot affected these ships was the design which allowed no ventilation. War ships were particularly susceptible, but cargo ships were not as liable to fungal attack as ventilation was allowed during loading and unloading. Dampness combined with a lack of correct ventilation provided perfect conditions for the germination and rapid growth of dry rot.

Many ideas for the curing of dry rot in ships were suggested. These included various chemical treatments which proved only marginally successful due to the impermeability of good oak. Another more successful method was to pack salt around the timbers, as salt-treated timber has a certain resistance to fungal decay.

A drastic method of treatment was to actually sink the ship and leave it submerged for several months in sea water on the assumption that this would pickle the timbers. The ship would then be re-floated. This method certainly killed off the fungal outbreak, but due to the density of the oak, did not give permanent resistance to decay, and rot reappeared very quickly.

Dry rot was always a problem in ships until the advent of iron constructed vessels. Obviously no nourishment could be derived from such a structure, so the fungus became purely dependent upon the wood still used in house construction for its survival.

Houses however did not suffer the same conditions of severe dampness as sea going ships, so homes built with good quality oak enjoyed a reasonable resistance to attack by dry rot. Inevitably oak soon became scarce and substitute timber had to be found. During the house-building boom of 1890-1910 most houses were constructed using soft woods and if timbers were allowed to become damp fungal decay soon followed.

It was during the Second World War that dry rot really became well known. House maintenance was largely neglected and defects which allowed the passage of dampness into buildings were ignored. Bomb damage, directly and indirectly, caused dry rot problems to the many thousands of homes affected in this way. Cracked gutters and rain-water pipes, missing roof tiles and broken windows allowed rainwater to seep through into the buildings.

Because of the fear of gas attack from the enemy, ventilation of houses was stopped, sub-floor ventilation was blocked up and no air was allowed into the timber cavity, thus causing the humidity to rise and resulting in massive dry rot outbreaks on a scale never before experienced.

Houses requisitioned by the army were a prime target for dry rot as, although minor repairs were carried out, major problems were mostly ignored.

For many years after the war, dry rot still raged. When requisitioned houses were given back to their owners, many were rife with dry rot and a number of lawsuits were brought against the government. However, the owner had to prove that the dry rot was not present before the government had taken possession.

This was difficult to prove, and resulted in most of these cases eventually failing in court. Today, with particular emphasis on insulation, we tend to neglect important ventilation in the mistaken belief that we are saving energy. It is the current trend to believe that heat should be saved at all costs. However this can cause many problems, not least in terms of condensation. With the popularity of double-glazing, draft excluders and cavity-wall insulation, we enclose ourselves in a bubble, which can cause condensation and result in black mould on the walls, pools of water on window sills and, even more damaging, the unseen menace – dry rot.

WHAT IS DRY ROT?

The fungi which cause the decay of timber in houses today can be classified into two groups, white rot, and brown rot.

WHITE ROT
This group of fungi belong to the group known as wet rot and is always characteristic of very high moisture content. White rot will cause decay by removing the lignin and cellulose from the wood, thus bleaching the timber. White rot is fairly easily diagnosed by the damage caused. It is not necessary to identify the exact type of fungus responsible for an attack as the treatment will consist of isolating the source of the dampness, removal and replacement of the decayed wood. White rot does not affect masonry and should not cause too much concern.

The species of white rot often encountered are:
Phellinus contiguus.
Pleurotus ostreatus.
Asterostroma spp.
Donkioporia expansa.

Phellinus contiguus is most common on external joinery, i.e. window frames, door frames. This is usually due to poor or cracked paintwork allowing water to seep into the wood.

When rotting by this fungus has occurred the damaged wood takes on a stringy appearance – it always reminds me of the breakfast cereal, Shredded Wheat. When tested between finger and thumb it does not powder but rolls into string. Sometimes a fruiting body can be seen, this is very tough and is usually dark brown in colour.

Treatment. Remove rotted sections of wood and replace. Ensure frames are well painted to avoid re-infestation.

Pleurotus ostreatus is a fungus that is usually found on hardwood trees. However in the home it tends to cause decay in chipboard when subjected to high moisture content, as from a plumbing or roof leak.

Treatment. Dry out affected area and replace as necessary.

Asterostroma spp affect softwoods and are usually found on joinery affected by dampness from plumbing leaks and, rarely, rising damp. As with *Phellinus contiguus*, the wood becomes stringy and does not rot into cuboid cracks as with dry rot.

This species of white rot does produce fungal strands and can cross very damp brickwork in search of food.

Treatment. Dry out affected area and replace as necessary.

Donkioporia expansa is found in oak timbers and is generally caused by water leaks. Wood becomes bleached and stringy. This fungus will soften the wood to allow a secondary infestation by death watch beetle. Therefore any survey carried out should include inspection of all timbers for this insect.

Treatment. Dry out affected area and replace timber as necessary. Carry out full inspection for death watch beetle. (For further information on death watch beetle, refer to *BRE Digest 307,* available from the Building Research Establishment, Bucknalls Lane, Garston, Watford, Herts)

BROWN ROT

Brown rot is a type of wood-rotting fungus that feeds only on the cellulose, and leaves the lignin intact. It therefore darkens the wood. The nutrients are absorbed by the fungus causing the wood to shrink and spit. This in turn will cause the characteristic cuboid cracking. Dry rot is a brown rot. Other species include, *Coniophora puteana* (cellar fungus), and *Fibroporia vaillantii*, (mine fungus) these can cause decay in wet conditions within buildings and exterior situations, commonly being confused with dry rot.

Dry rot affecting floor joists. To the left of this picture you can see a fruiting body just developing.

There is only one dry rot: *Serpula lacrymans.* . Dry rot is in itself a contradiction in terms, as initially the fungus will only occur in moist conditions where both the wood and atmosphere must be damp. The name 'dry rot' is probably due to the fact that this fungus can germinate at a lower moisture content than wet rot, and that the decay caused by the dry rot fungus renders the timber dry so that it crumbles readily into powder. Dry rot is also the only fungus that has the limited ability to transport water and cause decay in otherwise drier timber.

The fruiting body of dry rot is not of a standard size and can be as small as half an inch to several square feet when mature. The margin is white and swollen and surrounds a rust-coloured surface which is sometimes formed in a honeycombed manner. The rust coloration is due to the millions of spores waiting to be distributed into the air.

Spores are hardened containers which possess all the DNA instructions required to create a new fungus. They are in fact airborne floating eggs. If they bump into unsuitable materials such as dry wood or walls, they will just rebound and carry on floating, however when they bump into timber with the correct requirements, they will stick, and out of the opened shell a single fungus creature's body will appear, this is known as the germ tube. An arm grows from that body, from that arm grows another, and another, and then many many more. This will then form the hypha. Under the microscope

spores are yellow in colour, but red when viewed with the naked eye. These spores can be noticed on painted surfaces and resemble red dust, and if counted will be over one million spores to one square inch.

One average sized fruiting body (sporophore) of dry rot will distribute approximately 900 million spores per hour which is enough to infect every house in England. It is commonly accepted that every single house in Europe is infected by spores from dry rot which will germinate if given the correct conditions for growth, i.e. suitable food source, heat, humidity, moisture.

After the germination and establishment of dry rot, the conditions become a secondary factor, as dry rot has

a limited ability to transport water from a damp source in order to decay otherwise drier wood. The treatment of dry rot is not, therefore, a case of removing the moisture source, as the fungus will continue to survive for many years, only to be woken from its slumber if the correct dampness levels return.

Fruit bodies usually occur on walls, behind skirting boards, under sides of floor boards and occasionally on an outside wall. The fruit body itself may be regarded as marking the end of a fungal infestation in a particular direction, or a charging station from which renewed growth will occur.

The conditions that favour the growth and development of dry rot are temperature (ideal room temperature), moisture content of at least 21%, but more likely to be 28-30%, and humidity (lack of correct ventilation). The latter being the reason that dry rot is not found outside buildings. When spores land on any substance that is not wood, the spores cannot survive after the food source contained within the spore is exhausted and will eventually die of starvation. However, if the spores happen to land on wood which  has the correct moisture content, heat and humidity, then growth will usually occur.

When germination has occurred, the hypha is produced, this is a type of root which will penetrate into the wood and allow the fungus to absorb nourishment from the wood by producing enzymes which break down the wood structure and encourage further development

25

by producing the fungal mycelium. This will absorb all the necessary nourishment to promote healthy growth and development. The presence of the fungus will bring about complete changes in the substance and structure of the wood, giving no external evidence of its presence until severe rotting has occurred. The first structural sign of attack by dry rot is usually slight distortion of a skirting board or door frame, or maybe a slight drop in one corner of the floor, but by the time this sign is noticed, it is guaranteed that the infestation is well established and will require urgent and complete treatment to prevent further damage and expense.

In addition to the internal mycelium, there is usually an external growth resembling a white fluffy pad, like cotton wool, this depends on the amount of moisture available. At a later stage this growth may become compacted and become silvery grey resembling silk sheeting, often light purple. Toward the end of the 'sheet-like' growth, the mycelium is formed. The mycelium then produces fungal strands which travel from the wood in search of further nourishment and will grow over non food materials such as brickwork, concrete and behind plaster in search of more wood to add to the overall infestation. When the fungal strands grow over brickwork, they seem to do so with remarkable speed. This is possibly due to the fact that masonry offers no food value and therefore represents a hostile environment which must be crossed quickly. If these

A leaking water pipe causing a massive dry rot outbreak.

fungal strands do not find wood, they tend to die off leaving the main fungus to concentrate its search in other more productive areas in order to sustain further growth and development and to ensure the survival of the outbreak after the original food source has been exhausted.

When established, moisture levels are not crucial due as dry rot has its own limited water-making abilities which help to continue its growth into drier timbers. For those interested in the chemical breakdown, the water is

27

the result of metabolism with the conversion of hydrogen and oxygen which together with carbon are present within the wood.

When the fungi is established within a house and conditions are right, the fruiting body will then be produced. The presence of the fruiting body will always indicate that a severe dry rot outbreak has occurred and is well enough established to reproduce.

The production of the conducting strands which may be up to 6mm thick is characteristic of dry rot and may

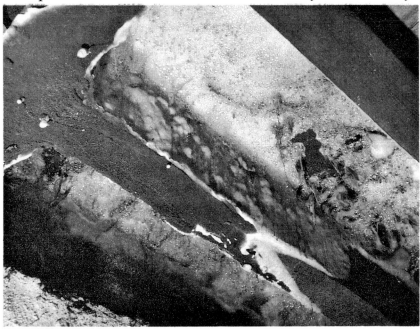

Active dry rot under the floor. This photograph clearly shows the droplets of water created by the fungus to enhance further growth.

extend for many feet over substances that cannot provide nourishment such as mortar joints, brickwork and masonry. A clear example of this is a recent survey that I carried out at a local hospital, where I was asked to trace and identify an outbreak of dry rot. The main fruiting body (sporophore) was on a brick wall of a basement, apparently being nourished by the bricks themselves! The ceilings were concrete and no timber was present within yards of the sporophore. This fruiting body was over one meter in diameter with no visible

Dry rot on a concrete wall. Although dry rot cannot absorb nourishment from masonry, it can us it as a passage to further sources of food.

means of support, however on carefully tracing the fungal strands, it became clear that the mycelium had grown through 15 feet of brickwork from a room with a timber floor which was unventilated and showed high levels of dampness. This is how a single outbreak of dry rot can grow in a terraced house and then extend through various party walls to affect several houses within the same terrace.

I am often asked to inspect properties with dry rot affecting a party wall and, in one instance, I became unwittingly involved in a legal issue.

The house in question was owned by a lady, Mrs Ford, who was most distressed to find large mushroom growths appearing from her staircase. On tracing the reason for this outbreak, I could not find any cause of dampness that would have caused such a problem, however at that time insurance companies would cover dry rot under the terms of the building policy. As no dampness problem could be detected, I had to presume that this outbreak had originated from the adjoining property which was a corner shop. After being given permission from Mrs Ford to discuss her dry rot problem with the owner of the adjoining property, I approached the shop-keeper who allowed me to inspect his premises. After lifting various floor boards and confirming the presence of the fungus, I traced the cause to a leaking cold water pipe under the store room.

I prepared full written reports for both properties

and, at their request, my technicians carried out the eradication treatment for Mrs Ford and the corner shop and subsequently issued guarantees for both properties.

A month later, I received a letter from a solicitor acting on behalf of Mrs Ford, who was suing the shop owner for damage due to the dry rot outbreak from his property, and requesting that I appear in court as an expert witness on her behalf. Apparently, Mrs Ford had made a claim on her building insurance policy, and, after a visit by the loss adjuster, the claim was refused as, according to my report, the fungal outbreak had originated from the adjoining property and was not therefore classed as a defect to the insured house. Mrs Ford was advised to take legal action to reclaim the cost of dry rot treatment and, as the shop owner was not insured, he was not covered.

I found myself in a very difficult position as both parties were my clients. Being bound by professional ethics, I refused and risked being held in contempt of court. Luckily, the case was settled out of court and I was not required to attend after all.

This experience taught me a very valuable lesson as to the responsibility of us all to ensure that our homes remain free of dry rot. If other properties become damaged from a rot outbreak originating from one house, that owner can be sued for the full amount of the remedial costs, and with recent changes in insurance policies, which can expressly exclude dry rot, this can be extremely expensive.

Dry rot can be very sensitive to temperature changes and will grow most rapidly at approximately 22°C, although it will still grow at temperatures ranging from just above 0°C to as high as 26°C, but will be killed if exposed to a temperature of over 40°C for a prolonged period. Dry rot is therefore restricted mainly to temperate climates, such as northern Europe and other colder areas. Dry rot is not found in the tropics, however a reference in the Bible (Leviticus, Chapter XIV) seems to contradict this. (See the history section of this book).

It is well known that dry rot does tend to become more virulent the further north you go, for example dry rot tends to be faster-growing and more damaging in Scotland than in southern England.

The amount of damage caused by dry rot in this country is far greater than most home owners would expect, although most of the damage can be avoided entirely by correct ventilation of the sub floor areas and periodic checking of plumbing, gutters and rain-water pipes. If a building is kept in good repair then there will be no need to fear the ravages of dry rot in your own home, although, of course, you have no control over dry rot that may invade from an adjoining property.

HOW TO RECOGNISE DRY ROT

The diagnosis of dry rot is sometimes not as straightforward as you might imagine, even for experienced surveyors.

My partner walked into my office covered in soot and dirt with a hurt look on his face.

"I was bloody trapped," he said.

He went on to explain that he was inspecting a house for rising dampness and during this inspection he had cause to inspect the basement.

"I was going down the basement steps and they bloody collapsed," he said.

"Why did they collapse?" I asked

"I had to climb out of the bloody coal hole," he replied.

I tried again: "Why did the staircase collapse?"

"I don't bloody know, they were bloody rotten," he snarled.

With that I packed my ladder into the car and drove to the house to inspect the offending basement. On arrival I found that the staircase had indeed collapsed and was completely decayed by dry rot, with the fungus extending to a large area of the ground floor. Fruiting bodies of the fungus were hanging from the walls under the late staircase and the air was pungent with the smell of fresh mushrooms.

This was by no means an isolated case, and the dry rot industry is ripe with similar stories. I once visited a friend who is a qualified F.R.I.C.S. (Fellow of the Royal

Institute of Chartered Surveyors). This poor chap told me that he had just returned from an inspection of a property in which he had been requested by the building society to prepare a full structural report. As he was pacing across his office floor dictating the report to his secretary, there was a dull splintering sound as the floor gave way, engulfing him to his waist in rotted floor boards. Just prior to his unfortunate mishap, he had been recommending a specialist dry rot investigation to be carried out on the house that he had just inspected.

To diagnose dry rot, we must firstly discuss and understand other types of fungi that can be confused with dry rot, these are known collectively as 'wet rot', and consist of several species that will cause decay in wood, all with their own characteristic decay pattern. To avoid confusion we will not go into details of the many different types of wet rot. For the time being we will deal only with the two most common species – cellar fungus, *Coniophora puteana*, and mine fungus, *Fibroporia vaillantii.*

Coniophora puteana **(cellar fungus)** is by far the most common of all wood-rotting fungi found in Britain today and requires higher moisture levels than dry rot for germination and continued growth. Timber affected by *Coniophora* can be darkened to appear almost black and can resemble charring, as if burnt. The visible damage to the wood consists of longitudinal splits with less pronounced cracking across the grain forming cuboid cracking. Another characteristic of this fungus is the presence of an apparently sound skin of veneer which can be easily peeled off to reveal the damaged wood. Due to the presence of this veneer, it can be difficult to tell if a section of timber is affected, and attention should be paid to any warping or twisting of the timber surface to identify an attack.

A property that I recently inspected was a good example of this. The house was built over an underground river which, at times of heavy rainfall, would flood into the oversites under the floor boards. The combination of flooding and poor sub-floor ventilation had resulted in severe wet rot damage to the entire

Wet rot of the type *Coniophora puteana*. This attack was due to a lack of ventilation under the timber floors.

ground floor area. On inspection of the sub-floor cavity it was clear that the joists were affected, but no immediate evidence of rotting was seen on the boards until I found myself sitting in a puddle looking up through a large person-shaped hole that I had made by falling through the floors. After scrambling back and dislodging more rotted timber, I found that all the floor boards were weakened and rotted, but were covered by the solid-looking veneer which had made the timbers appear sound.

The fungal strands are commonly found growing on the timbers and on adjacent brickwork in very wet conditions. Another area where I have commonly seen *Coniophora* strands is between a damp timber or concrete floor and linoleum. The fungal strands of *Coniophora* are usually dark brown, as opposed to the grey of dry rot.

The fruiting body of *Coniophora* is rarely found in buildings and consists of an olive green to brown plate. The smell tends to be musty and damp.

Fibroporia vaillantii (**mine fungus, white pore fungus**) can usually be identified by the presence of pure white mycelium, the characteristic decay pattern is very similar to that of dry rot but cuboid cracking is never as deep. This fungus, in my experience, is rarely found in buildings and is always associated with very high moisture levels, such as plumbing leaks.

Wet rot of the type *Fibroporia vaillantii*. This outbreak was caused by a leak from the washing machine.

THE CAUSES OF WET ROT

Before any treatment for wet rot can be considered, the cause of the dampness responsible must be identified. The most common cause of dampness are as follows.

Ground levels

The external ground level should be at least 6" below the damp proof course. A common problem is the laying of paths and driveways with no allowance for protecting the damp proof course. Also check soil levels and any walls adjoining the main structure, i.e. garden wall with no visible vertical damp proof course.

Rising Dampness

Moisture readings should be taken on all ground floor walls using a conductive meter. These meters are now available at very low cost at builders' merchants and hardware stores. Rising dampness may be present within the walls for many years before the staining on the wall-covering appears, so a moisture meter is a valuable addition to your tool box and will give an early warning of problems to come.

An electronic moisture meter works on the assumption that wet masonry or timber will conduct electricity better than dry. A moisture meter consists of two needle like probes which are used to pierce the plaster surface and to measure the conductivity between them, the better the conductivity, the higher the moisture level.

Rising dampness is not an easy defect to identify. The cause of any moisture meter reading can be influenced by secondary conditions, i.e. the presence of ground salts (chloride, nitrates, and sulphates) which could be present within the surface of the plaster finish and residual from a previous rising damp problem which has since been rectified.

Moisture readings are obtained from salt-contaminated plaster because of the ability of some ground salts to absorb moisture from the surrounding air. On days of high relative humidity, the salts will absorb moisture and deliquesce, which basically means that the salts have absorbed so much water that they actually turn liquid, thus giving a falsely high reading on the moisture meter scale. This characteristic of plaster to retain salts is the main reason why all remedial damp-proofing companies insist that plaster should be replaced at the same time as the installation of a damp proof course. A damp-proofing company will not usually be willing to issue a long-term guarantee unless the plaster is replaced.

Some types of building block will also give a false reading on a moisture meter through their ability to conduct electricity, i.e. carbon.

Another problem that I encounter is when the home owner has fixed tin foil to a wall prior to papering. When tested with a moisture meter, the reading will show maximum dampness due to the excellent conductivity of the metal. I have known damp-proofing companies to recommend complete damp-proof injection and associated re-plastering just because their moisture meter falsely indicated dampness.

When moisture readings appears on a conductivity meter, a good rule of thumb is to peel away a small section of wallpaper and inspect the plaster finish and then, if possible, take further moisture readings on the bare plaster. When the results are compared with the readings obtained from the wallpaper surface, they should read the same. If not, condensation could be the problem.

Another useful method to determine whether rising dampness is present is to lift a floor board and inspect the existing physical damp proof course, usually slate or bitumen. With the use of your meter, take a reading below and above the damp proof course. If high moisture readings are present, the readings are the same and there is no external evidence of moisture penetration, you can assume that there is rising dampness.

Any sources of moisture within the fabric of the building is cause for concern and should be investigated and cured to prevent fungal or insect damage to structural timbers.

Rising dampness is in my experience the most common cause of wet rot and is caused by either a breakdown or bridging of the existing damp proof course. This will cause moisture to rise from the ground by capillary action thus raising the moisture levels of masonry and adjacent timbers. Rising dampness can be cured by the installation of a chemical damp proof course and associated re-plastering to remove the salts deposited. A chemical damp proof course is best installed by a professional company as guarantees will be required should you sell the property in the future.

Before committing yourself to the expense of a new damp proof course, check that no bridging of the damp proof course has occurred, i.e. high ground level, adjoining garden walls have the correct vertical damp proof membrane or the presence of a plinth or rubble piled against the wall

Leaking gutters or rain–water pipes
Defective gutters or rain-water pipes are a common cause of wet rot and dry rot. Check brickwork for stains characteristic of leaks, i.e. green algae on walls. Pay particular attention to rain-water pipes, these can be easily blocked thus causing water to overflow from the joints which are not designed for coping with water rising up the pipes.

Plumbing defects
An inspection should be carried out of radiator valves and heating pipes. Particular attention should be paid to the rear of the WC, bathroom fittings and water mains inlet, usually found under the kitchen sink. Check the

seals on the bath or shower and make sure that water is not overflowing to hidden timber. Pay particular attention to the rear of the WC pan at the soil pipe join, this is a common cause of dampness.

Roofing leaks

Leaks from the roof can usually be traced from visual examination of the tiles/slates, or from inspection of timbers within the roof void. More difficult to determine are problems from flashing around chimneys and valleys. A reputable roofing specialist should be instructed to inspect and prepare a written quotation for necessary repairs.

Condensation

Condensation is caused whenever air containing a substantial amount of water is cooled below the temperature at which it is saturated. This temperature is known as the 'dew point'.

Air from outside, no matter how cold or wet the weather, will not cause condensation inside a building so long as the building is at least slightly warmer than the outside air.

Condensation can only be caused by water added to the air within the building. Washing, cooking, and drying clothes etc. add greatly to the air moisture. In addition to the activities of the occupants, water vapour can be bought into the building by wet clothes or other absorbent materials which will give up water to the warm air. Other sources of condensation include rising damp, penetrating damp, and residual water used in the construction of a property when constructed.

Condensation usually occurs at times when the water-making activities have finished, and the building begins to cool. This happens mostly in the late evening as the walls become colder and subsequently wet, causing mould quickly to appear.

Condensation is a major cause of both wet and dry rot. We have all experienced the visible condensation on windows and bathroom/kitchen tiles, however, more sinister is the condensation that we cannot see. This includes the build up of humidity under the floors due to the blocking or bridging of the sub-floor ventilation and the blocking of chimneys with no allowance for essential ventilation.

The sub-floor cavity requires at least one air change per hour which will mean that a sub-floor vent should be present at five feet that centres on all external walls to avoid the possibility of a rise in moisture content to the timbers. Should the moisture content rise to above 21% then dry rot is a possibility. Wet rot will require higher moisture levels. Poor sub-floor ventilation is a common cause of dry rot.

One very common problem encountered is the building of an extension at the rear of a house, completely blocking sub-floor ventilation of floor timbers. Such extensions tend to be built with solid floors and with no thought given to the damage that will be caused to the timber floors of the original building by the complete lack of an underfloor through draft.

When chimneys are no longer required for coal fires, we tend to brick up and not allow ventilation. The problems arise when no allowance is made for ventilation and humidity will start to increase. This excess moisture will combine with the soot (sulphates) within the flue and migrate to the surface of the chimney breast, sometimes causing stained damp patches. This moisture can cause adjacent timbers to become damp leaving the timbers open to attack by fungus and wood boring insects.

Penetrating dampness
Penetrating dampness can be classified as any moisture penetration into the fabric of the building other than rising dampness and condensation. Penetrating dampness can be caused by defective roofing, poor pointing, cracked or defective rendering, leaking and defective or blocked down pipes and gutters

THE CURE OF WET ROT

When the dampness problem has been identified and cured, the cure of the wet rot can commence.

Firstly, remove damaged portions of the timbers to at least 25 centimetres past the last evidence of fungal infestation.

Install the new pre-treated timbers taking care not to allow the damp masonry to come into contact with the new timbers through the use of a proprietary damp proof course membrane.

Adjacent timbers should be treated by the application of two brush coats of a fungicide/insecticide. This will offer complete protection to the timbers during the drying time. When masonry has been allowed to become damp, the drying time can be approximately one month per inch thickness of the wall, therefore a nine-inch wall will take nine months to dry.

There will be no need to treat adjacent masonry as the wet rot fungus will die once the timber dries and remains dry. However adjacent timbers must be treated to protect them during the drying period.

Recently, I was asked to carry out a survey on a large ground floor flat in south-west London where the presence of dry rot had been confirmed and quotations ranging between £7,000 and £8,000 had been given by various specialist companies.

During my inspection there was no evidence of dry rot in any part of the property and, although wood damage was apparent to some floors due to fungal infestation, it was entirely due to wet rot of the type *Fibroporia vaillantii*, and not a major problem. My estimate for remedial treatment was £800, just 10% of the quotations received from the other 'specialist' companies.

This leads me to the problem of mis-diagnosis. During the course of my work, I am often given copies of the pre-purchase building society valuer's report on the condition of a particular property, many times I have read: "Possibilities of wet/dry rot within this property, we recommend that a full report is obtained from a specialist company."

It is very rare that problems exist, but if a valuer observes a defect that could indicate the presence of dry rot, he will usually cover himself by passing the buck to a commercial organisation that would like nothing more than to find dry rot.

Frequently remedial companies and specialist surveyors will, if in any doubt as to the nature or recognition of a fungus, report it as dry rot – just to be safe!

This could be for various reasons, the first being that the surveyor has not the experience or the knowledge to identify the correct species of fungus. The second and more common reason is that dry rot treatment offers a greater profit potential than wet rot, and a surveyor working for a commercial company will generally wish to bring in the greatest value of contract possible.

An active outbreak of dry rot will always be expensive due to the nature of this fungus and its ability to colonise masonry as well as timbers. The treatment required will mean exposing the full extent of the outbreak and continuing at least a further one metre past the last evidence to ensure full exposure. The next step is to sterilise all of the adjacent timbers and masonry.

Wet rot will usually confine its activities to wet timber and will not use masonry as a route to further food sources, therefore, it is usually sufficient to identify and cure the cause of fungal infestation and replace timbers as affected.

THE IDENTIFICATION OF DRY ROT

To rule out the possibility of wet rot, and confirm correctly the presence of dry rot, the following rules should apply.

Smell

When dry rot is actively growing, a strong mushroom odour will always be present in the area of attack, this should not be confused with the musty smell associated with wet rot.

Recently, I heard about dogs being specially trained to sniff out dry rot in houses, these are perhaps a variation of the truffle hounds of France!

Presence of fruiting body

If a fruiting body is found in any area, then dry rot is definitely present. This is usually the first sign that most home owners encounter. However, my aim is to teach people to recognise dry rot before the formation of the sporophore, by which widespread damage will have already occurred.

Fruiting bodies will occur almost anywhere inside the building, and sometimes on an outside wall. Many times I have seen these growths on carpets, growing

Dry rot strands under a timber floor. These strands are used to grow through or over masonry to search for additional food sources.

behind wardrobes and in cupboards, however, the fruiting body will occur most frequently within a floor cavity and at the site of the damage.

Red dust

The presence of red dust within a property will always indicate dry rot. Due to the many millions of spores produced by dry rot, it is inevitable that some dust will settle in the vicinity of a sporophore. This dust will be found on window sills, tops of light switches, plug sockets and anywhere that normal household dust might settle.

Dry rot fruiting body growing from between the skirting board and floor. Note the warping of the skirting board.

This staircase collapsed during normal use. The dry rot was not seen until the exposure was carried out

Another interesting point about the dry rot fungus is its ability to produce larger, or additional sporophores when under stress. That is to say that if the food source has been exhausted, or a sub-lethal dose of fungicide has been applied, it will react by distributing as many seeds as possible into the air thus ensuring new outbreaks elsewhere and continuing the survival of the species.

Fungal strands

The presence of the fungal strands is one of the most important early warning signs and will confirm dry rot, given the other evidence associated with the presence of these strands.

The strands of dry rot will range in size from fine cotton, to the thickness of a pencil, becoming brittle when dry. The mycelium may appear as a silky grey sheet on the timber surface and in unventilated areas can resemble cotton wool. The fungal strands will not be seen in a ventilated area but will always be confined to the dark, damp places.

Visual damage to timbers

All brown rots including dry rot will cause cuboid splitting in timber. However the size of the cubes is usually the relevant factor in the diagnosis of dry rot. As mentioned previously, cellar fungus will produce pronounced longitudinal cracks with shallower splits across the grain and will generally produce smaller

Dry rot growing from a solid mosaic floor into the door frame.

cracks. Always bear in mind the presence of the solid-looking veneer associated with this fungus.

· *Fibroporia* (mine fungus) is easily confused with dry rot as the visual cuboid cracking is very similar. However it rarely is as deep.

Mine fungus will always be associated with the presence of pure white strands which are flexible when dry. It requires a much higher moisture content than is needed for the growth of dry rot, and is usually caused by an on-going plumbing leak.

Dry rot damage will consist of large cuboid cracking

caused by equal splitting of the wood along and across the grain, the timber will crumble readily into powder when rubbed between finger and thumb. Grey fungal strands will usually be present both on the surface and within the damaged timber.

VISUAL INDICATIONS OF PROBLEMS

The following visual indications could indicate the presence of dry or wet rot, and when encountered should be fully investigated.

Warping or shrinking of timbers will always be cause for concern because of the ability of rot to absorb the nourishment from the wood and cause shrinking. This effect will especially be encountered on painted surfaces like skirting boards, window frames, sills, and door frames. The paintwork surface will in effect hide the characteristic cuboid splitting and the fungal strands. A periodical inspection should be made to all skirting boards within a home to identify any slight distortion, and if encountered, the skirting board should be removed and the unpainted rear side inspected for any signs of rotting or strands.

I have found many dry rot outbreaks by checking the painted surfaces for signs of distortion, and it is an essential part of my survey on any property.

Another cause for concern will be **any sudden drop in the floors**. This can usually be quickly identified by any excessive bounce, or by periodic inspections of the gap between the floor boards and base of the skirting board. Although floor drop can indicate the presence of dry rot, it will more often be due to wet rot, woodworm attack or even a slight settlement of the sleeper walls. However, even if you don't suspect a major problem, just lift a floor board and with the use of a torch and a mirror, inspect the joist ends and plates. A five minute job could save you worry and expense.

Dry rot affecting floors and window frames. Note the external ground level is the same height as the internal floor, therefore bridging the damp proof course.

A TYPICAL SURVEY

At this point, I think it may be wise to take the reader through a typical survey, pointing out the basic procedures to confirm or rule out the possibility of dry rot.

Most dampness problems that cause dry rot can be identified from thorough visual inspection of the external face of the building.

External inspection

Prior to the internal survey, a complete visual inspection should be undertaken to reveal any likely causes of dampness that could cause internal decay.

1. Look at the overall condition of the roof, note any missing or broken tiles. Pay attention to the chimneys – are they open or capped? If blocked, condensation can build up within the flue and cause dampness to filter through brickwork to adjacent timbers.
2. Carry out a full inspection of the gutters, rain-water pipes and hopper heads. Defective or blocked guttering and rain-water pipes are a major cause of dry rot. Pay particular attention to any staining on the walls under gutters or beside rain-water pipes.
3. Check the window frames and sills. Note any staining under the windows and make sure that the drip throat is clear so that rain-water can run away from the brickwork. A drip throat is a groove

in the under-sides of the window sill which prevents rain-water from running down the wall.

4. Inspect the condition of the sub-floor vents – are they blocked? A common defect in the sub-floor vents is excessive painting. The grids may have had so many coats of paint over the years that they cannot do the job for which they were intended . There should be at least one sub-floor vent in every five feet of wall which should allow at least one air change per hour.

5. Make sure that the external ground level is at least six inches below damp proof course level.

If any defects are observed during the inspection of the above, then rot is a possibility.

Internal inspection.
Care should be taken to inspect areas likely to be affected by plumbing defects, the WC is a major culprit for leaks, especially from the joint between the pan and soil pipe.

The seal around the bath or shower should be inspected and confirmed watertight. The bath panel should be removed to check for leaks from the waste.

Any staining around radiator valves should be fully investigated. These valves frequently leak and are a major cause of rot.

Moisture readings should be taken on all walls using a conductive moisture meter, this will identify any damp areas and will point to possible trouble areas.

Any areas of dampness adjacent to timber should be thoroughly investigated, and in the case of timber floors, floor boards should be lifted and joists inspected with the aid of a torch and mirror. This will allow you to see a great deal of the underfloor area with the lifting of only one or two boards. Again I must point out the significance of any red dust encountered, if red dust is present, then dry rot has become established and will require urgent treatment.

THE EXTENT OF THE PROBLEM

If you are unfortunate enough to find dry rot during your inspection, the following procedure should be followed.

As the first evidence of the dry rot will usually be found on, or close to, timber, the affected wood should be removed to estimate the direction in which the fungus has spread.

It will not at this stage be necessary to hack off plaster, but is advisable to remove small squares of plaster at random in the suspect area. This will allow you to see the fungal mycelium on the bare brickwork behind, and get a fair idea of the direction in which it has grown.

Timber window frames, door frames and other joinery should be checked for any signs of distortion and with the aid of a bradawl or small screw driver. Pierce the surface; if the timber is soft then dry rot could be present, if the bradawl sticks into the timber and resists being removed, then it can be assumed that the timber is sound.

Once you are fairly confident of the extent of the outbreak, treatment can begin.

HOW TO TREAT
DRY ROT

It is important at this stage to point out that due to the specialist nature of dry rot eradication, it is not recommended that you undertake large scale treatment yourself. The reason for including this chapter is not so much to encourage DIY, but to give the home owner the knowledge to judge if a quotation received from a specialist company for the necessary work is reasonable, and to be confident of the ability to ensure that any works are being carried out correctly and competently.

Until recently, dry rot treatment was carried out by builders who did not understand the problems associated with eradicating this fungus. **The most common treatment was heat**, which involved the use of blow lamps to burn away surface mycelium in the hope that this would destroy the outbreak. However, due to the insulating effect of brickwork, and the ability of dry rot to penetrate deeply into the wall, this treatment did little or no good and dry rot frequently reappeared with a vengeance.

A more dramatic treatment, using heat to sterilise

brickwork, was proposed to the Ministry of Works in a paper dated January 1947, by Mr A. Habberstrad of Oslo, Norway. Electric hot plates could be used to sterilise masonry which had been in contact with the dry rot fungi. This method of heat treatment seemed to present a practical way of dealing with a small area of infected wall, and had the merit of being portable, with no fire risk.

Mr Habberstrad's invention was to be of sufficient interest to justify tests at public expense. These tests were carried out by the Building Research Station, in conjunction with The Forest Products Research Laboratory.

The apparatus consisted of an electric hot plate weighing 123lb, and having a maximum current consumption of 3.5 kW. The aim of this equipment was to raise the temperature of the wall to at least 40°C (104°F), thus killing the dry rot and drying out the wall.

A trial was carried out on a 13^1/$_2$ inch brick wall in which blocks of wood infected with dry rot were embedded. Temperature readings were taken from within the wall, and the opposite side to the heater.

The conclusions reached were as follows:
1. With the heater running at full capacity of 3.5 kW for sixteen hours or more the treatment would be successful in eradicating dry rot infection from an area not exceeding one metre square (the size of the heater).

2. With a single heater in operation the treatment showed no sign of damaging the brickwork. A battery of smaller heaters operating side by side, might produce a more damaging effect to the wall due to relative movement of heated and unheated areas.

This method of treatment never really caught on, and was forgotten in favour of chemical treatment. However with more and more public awareness of dangerous chemicals and their effects on our environment, it just may contribute to methods of treating dry rot in the future.

Another successful method of treatment was to expose the full extent of the fungal outbreak, take away any affected timber in the area, remove wall plaster, cure the moisture source, and leave fully exposed until the fungus starved to death. This method was successful but, due to the amount of time required for complete drying, it was not really practical.

The most successful treatment for dry rot is now accepted to be by chemical means and should proceed as follows. First and most important is to trace and cure the moisture source responsible for the decay – common causes of dampness are listed in Chapter 3.

EXPOSURE OF THE FUNGUS

Once the dampness source has been located and cured, exposure can begin. This is the most important part of the eradication treatment as no cure can begin until the full extent of dry rot growth is known.

Exposure of a dry rot fungus is usually carried out by a specialist company, as they will be more experienced in determining the direction of growth and distance of spread. If you feel confident about exposing the outbreak yourself, then it is absolutely vital to observe the following procedure.

First remove all affected timber to at least one metre past the last sign of decay or softness and remove from the house immediately. The affected wood should be burnt as soon as practicable.

When you are confident that all decayed timber has been removed and cut back to at least one metre past the last visible evidence of infection, then exposure of brickwork can begin.

Carefully remove plaster to expose the fungal strands that will be present on the brickwork. This will allow a visual inspection of the area of infection. Once the brickwork is exposed, you will usually see the fungal mycelium. This will resemble grey or off white cobwebs. Pay attention to the direction in which the stronger strands are growing and make note. Continue to remove the plaster in all directions of the outbreak, following the fungal strands until you are satisfied that all fungal mycelium has been exposed, after which a further 600mm of plaster in all directions beyond the last evidence should be removed as an additional safety measure .

During the exposure works, you may find that some of the fungal strands have achieved their objective and found additional timber, In this case, the exposure works will have to begin again from the site of the additional outbreak following the same procedure. If the fungal strands seem to cease in close proximity to a dividing or party wall, do not be complacent, floors should be lifted and plaster removed from the other side, you must be ruthless now as just a small amount fungus remaining could cause enormous problems at a later date.

The exposure of the *full* extent of dry rot is absolutely necessary, and could mean the removal of staircases, fully-fitted kitchen units and other valuable fixtures. There are no short cuts and affected areas must in all cases be exposed.

A point worth mentioning at this stage is the practice of some specialist dry rot companies to issue a quotation only for exposure of the fungal outbreak, then when full exposure is complete, an additional quotation is issued depending on the extent of the growth found. Due to the nature of dry rot, the full extent of growth cannot be accurately determined at the time of the initial survey. However, if a surveyor is experienced in the identification of dry rot, he should be able to estimate maximum expected growth by using his judgement and experience of similar situations and therefore give a fairly accurate estimation of expected cost. Be careful of companies that are not willing to commit themselves to a rough estimate of costs prior to work beginning. If they are only quoting for exposure they may over-expose, leading to a higher charge for treatment and reinstatement.

You are of course not obliged to accept the further quotation after exposure, but you may find other companies unwilling to continue treatment started by someone else, and they may be reluctant to issue a long-term guarantee based on preparation works carried out by others.

Dangers of under-exposure
Exposure of a serious dry rot outbreak can be heart-breaking, as the need for removal of anything in its path is most important and absolutely necessary.

A few years ago, I was instructed to inspect a large country house where dry rot was reported to be affecting two door frames of the ballroom, thought to be due to a burst water tank in the loft. On inspection of this property the ballroom was an exquisite example of Georgian elegance. Crystal chandeliers hung from hand painted ceilings depicting cherubs on landscape. The walls were lined with hand-carved oak panels, and floors of Italian marble. The owner pointed out the door frames in question, which were indeed severely affected by dry rot. The problem here was that the affected door frames were 30 feet apart with no visual evidence of any dry rot on any timber between the two, except one very small fruiting body appearing from the base of the timber cladding halfway between the two rotted frames. I explained to the shocked owner that in my opinion, the damage to both areas was due to one outbreak, and treatment would involve exposing all walls between the visually affected areas and perhaps further. This was not acceptable to the owner and after listening to my reasoning, refused to accept that such drastic exposure was necessary with so small an amount of visual damage. Instead he employed an odd job man who subsequently replaced only the affected door frames. I feared for this house and was not surprised when two years later I was called back by the owner who was now resigned to major works. When I saw this ballroom for the second time I was surprised and saddened at the extent to which the dry rot had grown. The new door frames had rotted and the timber panels had cracked and were being pushed away from the walls by the huge amount of fungus behind. Fruiting bodies were growing from the wall/ceiling joint, and approximately half the room was now visually affected by dry rot.

Full exposure was at last carried out, and the dry rot cured, but at considerably greater cost, both for remedial treatment and loss of irreplaceable fixtures.

The majority of this expense and loss could have been avoided by the courage and determination to deal comprehensively with the problem as soon as it became known.

TREATMENT AND STERILISATION

Once the exposure is complete, the moisture source responsible for the decay cured, and the full extent of fungal infestation is known the chemical treatment can then commence.

Preparation and cleaning

Remove as much of the surface mycelium as possible and thoroughly clean down the exposed brickwork using a wire brush.

Fungicide

Spray all exposed. masonry and oversites using a fungicidal wall solution. It is not necessary to go into details of the active ingredients of these fungicides, but ·it should be pointed out that they are toxic, so appropriate safety equipment must be used, i.e. face mask and goggles, gloves and overalls. The spray should be applied in accordance with the manufacturer's instructions on the container and allowed to dry.

Irrigation

The process of irrigation, known as the 'toxic box', is carried out to provide a barrier, or *cordon sanitaire*, around

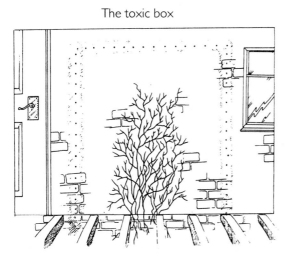

The toxic box

an actively-growing area of dry rot, thus containing the growth to a selected area of brickwork or unaffected timber. This is achieved by drilling a series of holes, 10mm in diameter, to two thirds of the depth of the wall around the fungal outbreak. These holes are then injected with the necessary chemical, thus saturating the wall and providing a chemical block throughout the full depth. Until recently the method used to treat masonry affected by dry rot was to drill and inject every brick. However, on tests carried out by the relevant authorities it was proved that the chemical did not penetrate sufficiently into the brickwork to sterilise, so that full irrigation of every brick in an affected area is now thought to be completely unnecessary and could in fact introduce more unwanted water into an already damp wall thus prolonging the drying period. When sterilisation treatment has been completed, the dry rot outbreak should be successfully cured and reinstatement can commence.

Timber replacement

Ideally, all replacement timber should be pre-treated (timber treated using pressure or vacuum impregnation of preservatives prior to sale). Take care to coat any timbers after cutting, using two coats of fungicide.

If pre-treated timber is not available, then new timber should be treated using an organic solvent wood preservative by two liberal brush coats prior to fixing.

Existing unaffected timbers should be sprayed using an organic solvent wood preservative in accordance with the manufacturer's instructions, this treatment should be applied to both surface and under-sides of floors and should include joists and floor plates.

Replacement of plaster

The first and second coats should be 4-1 sulphate-resisting cement and washed river sharp sand. The use of sharp sand will allow the mortar to become workable with the addition of the minimum amount of water. Too much water added to the mortar will result in excessive shrinkage during drying, and can cause cracking when dry. Plasticisers can be used but remember not to use washing liquid as is common practice, this contains salt and could cause problems. Finish using multi-finish and trowel smooth.

Alternative plastering can be carried out using ZOC plaster (Zinc Oxychloride). This plaster has been specially developed to form a barrier which is toxic to the fungus, and can be obtained from The Preservation Centre for Wood, 24 Ossory Road, London SE1 5AN.

Always leave at least a one inch gap between a solid floor and the plaster, this will avoid any bridging of the damp proof course.

Decorating
Permanent redecoration should not be done until walls are thoroughly dry. This could take many months, but is usually within 10-12 weeks. Temporary decoration can be carried out using a matt emulsion which will allow the new plaster to breath during the drying process.

SELECTING A COMPANY

Recommendation or local reputation is usually the best to select a company to give you a quotation. However, Yellow Pages or the local Thomson directory is the method most commonly used.

During your initial enquiry, you should ask if the surveyor to visit you is qualified. If so, he should have the necessary letters after his name – C.R.D.S. (Certificated Remedial Damp Proofing Surveyor) or C.T.I.S. (Certificated Timber Infestation Surveyor). Be careful as it is the practice of some companies to send out a surveyor with very little specialist knowledge to inspect a problem These surveyors usually work on commission, so it is in their interest to make a problem look as bleak as possible. I know of several companies that employ untrained surveyors, who after maybe one week of experience with a qualified person, are let loose on the unsuspecting home owners, masquerading as specialists.

THE SURVEY
During the course of a survey for dry rot, the surveyor should first confirm the presence of dry rot. When this has been done, the surveyor should then trace the cause of dampness responsible for the fungal outbreak. This will involve internal and external examinations, perhaps even removing floor boards to check for plumbing leaks.

The next stage of a survey will be for the surveyor to use his skill and judgement to estimate the severity of the attack. Ideally, the surveyor should be allowed to remove skirting boards, floor boards, and small sections of plaster to determine the direction of growth from the visual outbreak. Once the surveyor is satisfied that the full extent of the outbreak is known, then the process of quoting for the cure can commence.

THE QUOTATION
A quotation issued from a specialist company should be broken down under five headings.

1. Cost of isolating and rectifying the dampness

source responsible for the decay and identifying and curing any other dampness sources that could cause problems in the future.

2. Cost of exposing the full extent of the fungal infestation by removal and disposal of decayed timber, and affected plaster, masonry, fixtures and fittings.

3. Cost of chemical sterilisation treatment to walls, oversites and existing sound timbers.

4. Cost of re-plastering of all walls exposed during the works.

5. Cost of replacing all affected timber, fixtures and fittings.

I have seen quotations from companies who will not break down the costs involved in treatment of a dry rot outbreak, and will only issue a total cost. This should not be acceptable as you need to know a breakdown of the individual costs in order to judge if, in your opinion, it is reasonable. For example, a recent report that I was shown just indicated a total cost with no evidence of how the total figure was determined. After speaking to the company concerned it was discovered that over £1,200 was for exposure only. This was unreasonable and was therefore refused by the client.

Many companies have in recent years got away with excessively high prices through the public's ignorance of the nature of dry rot. However, given ample information as to the proposed treatment involved and a proper breakdown of the charges, the client would soon realise that they were being overcharged. Another quotation that was shown to me recently allowed £800 for re-plastering four square metres which was obviously excessive, but this element might never have been picked up in 'total cost' quotation.

THE GUARANTEE

It is the recognised practice for all remedial companies to issue a long-term guarantee after the completion of works. This guarantee is issued because the company is confident about the quality of the work and is prepared to agree to rectify any re-infestation free of charge.

However, a guarantee should be read carefully as some will limit the liability to the cost of the original contract, which could mean that if a problem re-occurs, then the company is only liable for a fraction of the actual cost of re-treating.

Any guarantee is only as secure as the issuing company. Many times I have spoken to clients who assure me that guarantees are in force, but the company has gone out of business. The solution to this problem is now offered by all reputable companies, who will issue their own guarantee, but in addition will offer to underwrite the guarantee through an independent insurance company, a small charge may be required for this facility, but will always be worthwhile.

MY PROFESSIONAL OPINION

In this final chapter I will throw caution to the wind and describe some of my personal theories with regard to the dry rot fungus.

I am not a scientist but a surveyor working on the front line against this damaging fungus. It may, therefore, be felt that I am being presumptuous to include my own ideas, but many of them are based on experience directly related to actual dry rot outbreaks, and not to laboratory experiments.

I can honestly say that I have never seen a dry rot outbreak which has been caused exclusively by rising damp. Dampness rising from the ground is always contaminated by salts (chlorides and nitrates) therefore, as dry rot requires a slightly acid environment for germination to occur, these salts, being alkali, should restrict germination of the dry rot spore.

It is possible for rising dampness to cause dry rot but only indirectly. This occurs when a wall is subject to rising dampness and, in addition, the sub-floor ventilation within the property is blocked or restricted.

The moisture will then evaporate from the damp wall thereby raising the humidity within the sub-floor cavity. As timbers become wet from this condensation then dry rot could well erupt.

In my experience the main causes of dry rot are plumbing and gutter leaks. Defective plumbing is the prime cause of dry rot in houses today and is the most damaging as leaks are usually hidden under floors, behind sink units, and other concealed areas. Defective gutters or rainwater pipes allowing rainwater to pour onto external brickwork is a sure sign that there is a possibility of dry rot. The advantage with this type of dampness is that it can be easily spotted from the outside of the building, and quickly cured before too much damage has occurred.

Some specialists will insist that dry rot has the ability to grow from a damp to a dry area, using some sort of internal plumbing system to spread throughout the whole house, destroying everything in its path. This alarmist theory has obviously been cultivated by firms who until now have made a great deal of money from public ignorance of what is basically a localised building defect. Certainly, it has been proved that dry rot fungus can live for over four years in dry timber, and grow again if conditions become appropriate. However, if these conditions of dampness recur, an entirely new fungal outbreak is quite likely in any case.

The growth of dry rot can only continue whilst a

moisture source is present and will eventually die when all dampness is removed. Many theories exist as to the ability of dry rot to create its own water supply and continue to grow regardless of the fact that the dampness source has been stopped. Dry rot does indeed have a limited ability to create water, however this is unlikely to be enough to attack dry areas. Therefore after the infestation has run its course or dried out, it will not become dormant. It will eventually die, and the chances of re-infestation are then no greater than those of any previously unaffected timbers which are kept dry and ventilated.

We are told by the relevant authorities that dry rot will grow at a maximum rate of 15.8mm, or less than one inch, per week. This translates to under one metre per year. I have monitored a property affected by a dry rot outbreak over a period of six months. This property was owned by a building society who had repossessed. I was asked by the surveyors to inspect a small rot outbreak within the basement area. During my survey, one joist was found to be affected by fungal mycelium within the specified area, this had spread from the skirting board above and was caused by a slight leak from the central heating system together with a complete lack of ventilation within the basement. I duly submitted my report to the owners with a strong recommendation for urgent action, however my advice was ignored and the property was subsequently put on the market for

The basement ceiling, covered with white mycelium.

sale. Six months passed with no word, until one day the estate agent acting for the building society contacted me and asked if I would re-inspect. When I returned to the property, the dry rot in the basement had travelled 15 feet from the original source and the ceiling was completely covered with masses of white mycelium (as in the photograph above) which I had to remove before the timbers could be inspected. The floor above had rotted in two rooms and massive damage had occurred to door and window frames. The rate of growth was

Millions of fungal spores concentrated around a fruiting body.

astounding and I would never have believed that this was the same house that I had inspected only six months earlier. Before writing my report, I made enquiries to the estate agent as I thought there must have been some severe flooding to cause such rampant growth. The agent told me that after my original visit, the building society instructed a specialist company to carry out treatments which consisted only of fungicidal treatment to exposed timber. During the course of this work no exposure of the outbreak was carried out, no work was done to improve the ventilation to the basement and no masonry sterilisation was attempted.

In my opinion the treatment used to attempt a cure had caused the fungus to go into stress conditions thereby growing at many times the recognised rate. This stress factor has been noted by many specialists but the causes are not fully understood. Stress can, however, be caused by treating an outbreak with a sub-lethal dose of preservative or if a food source has been exhausted.

Stress caused by poison (sub-lethal fungicide treatment) is thought to be due to the ability of some types of fungus to absorb toxic substances encountered during its wanderings and to survive the poisons by releasing them into the air thus leaving the main fungal growth to continue at accelerated speeds. This stress factor has never been accepted by the relevant authorities, who seem to discount the theory as pure speculation. I have on many occasions seen dry rot which is under stress, for whatever reason, growing at many times the recognised rate. This causes many problems with diagnosis, not least in the many legal battles coming to court every year where the age of the dry rot outbreak is usually determined by the amount of growth. An independent witness assessing the age of a dry rot outbreak, stating the expected growth rate of only 15.8mm per week as per the guidelines laid down by the BRE, could be many years adrift.

A particularly interesting picture. During building works to this property a new floor screed was laid. However, hardcore used by the builder was affected by dry rot, which is here seen growing from the floor in search of suitable timber.

ACKNOWLEDGEMENT

During the writing of this book I carried out my research using old books, historic newspaper clippings and basically anything relevant to the subject that I could lay my hands on. As a working surveyor and not an academic, most of the information contained within the book comes from personal experience of dry rot and information gleaned from various publications over the years. Much of the information proved to be outdated and in some cases inaccurate. I therefore sought the advice of the following specialists whose criticism was most useful in weeding out the fact from the fiction.

I would like to thank Dr Carey, from the Building Research Establishment, for reading my original script and for advice on the biology of dry rot. I am also most grateful to the Institute of Wood Science, in particular to Jean Taylor (president of the Institute 1986-88), who gave me her time to assist in the preparation of the final script for publication.

My wife Alexandra not only encouraged me with the research and writing of the script, but also used her skills as a cartoonist to provide the line drawings contained in the book.